Longman Nature Guides

KU-157-421

Rocks

REFERENCE
FOR USE IN THE LIBRARY ONLY

Titles in the series:

Clouds and Weather

Butterflies and Moths of Britain and Europe

Longman Group Limited
*Longman House, Burnt Mill, Harlow,
Essex CM20 2JE, England*

Originally published in German by
Gräfe und Unzer GmbH, München
© by Gräfe und Unzer GmbH, München

English language edition © Longman Group Limited 1986

First published by Longman Group Limited 1986

British Library Cataloguing in Publication Data

Rocks.—(Longman nature guides)
1. Rocks
552   QE431.2

ISBN 0-582-89272-4

Set in Monophoto Photina by
Servis Filmsetting Limited, Manchester

Printed in Great Britain
by Blantyre Printing Co. Ltd., Blantyre.

Author: Hochleitner

Picture acknowledgements: all photographs by
the author.

Introduction

Rocks are everywhere, in town and country. In the open air they form cliffs and mountains, they occur as pebbles in every river, and in inhabited areas they are constituents of many buildings. Every day we meet rocks in a number of forms. If you park your car at the kerb or drive over cobbles, you are dealing with rocks, usually granite. Many buildings in London are made of Portland stone (limestone); in the Cotswolds the local stone (oolitic limestone) is used in building, in Aberdeen granite. All these materials are types of rock. Sand, gravel, slate, are other examples of rock familiar to everybody.

This book contains illustrations and descriptions of the most important types of rock. About two-thirds of these you can find in the British Isles, ranging from the chalk cliffs of Dover to the basalt columns of the Giant's Causeway in Northern Ireland. A large part of these islands is composed of common sedimentary rocks (sandstone, limestone, etc.), but metamorphic rocks (schist, gneiss, etc.) predominate north of the Firth of Forth, and a variety of igneous rocks (granite, basalt, etc.) may be found in Scotland, Wales, Ireland, and southwest England. Of the other rocks described, there are several which you may encounter in a worked form (e.g. obsidian used as a semiprecious stone, or pumice as a household abrasive), and others which you may well come across when travelling in Europe.

What is rock?

A rock is a naturally occurring body consisting of minerals of different kinds (or sometimes of a single kind) and varying in size from metres to kilometres. A rock can be so fine-grained that the individual mineral particles can be recognised only under the microscope, or so coarse-grained that individual grains reach a size of several metres. The constituents of a rock may be firmly bonded, as in granite and marble; but a rock may also, like sand or gravel, be made up of many movable particles (i.e. sand grains or pebbles in the present case). The external shape of a rock is determined by its environment and is only to a limited extent characteristic of its species. A rock can form a mountain or fill a crack in the country rock. It be broken to pieces or disintegrated into particles by weathering it is still a rock, irrespective of its external shape. A rock can also consist of fragments of other rocks, as in the case of gravel and conglomerates or breccia.

The great variety of rocks on our planet may seem bewildering. By offering a means of simple and reliable identification of many rocks, this book aims to help the amateur geologist and anyone interested in our natural environment.

Advice to the rock-collector

Where do you find rocks? Where are they most accessible? The entire earth is made of rocks, and therefore they can be collected everywhere where the topmost layer of the earth has been worn away or was never present. The collector may find particularly favourable conditions in quarries or large city building-sites, since here the rock tends to be recently exposed and not changed by weathering. Rocks may also be found in cliffs, scree slopes, and in freshly dug fields.

The geological specimens which you take home should all show important features of a rock. If the rock is very fine-grained, a relatively small piece is enough to show the structure and all constituents. On the other hand, you will need a much larger piece of coarse-grained granite to show all its features. If the feldspar in thi rock is 10cm in size, a piece measuring 10 × 5cm can never represent the entire rock. The specimens usually cut are rectangular, measuring 9 × 12cm (about the size of a hand). A good rock collec tion should if possible contain all the formations of a species of rock i.e. not only one type of granite but a variety of types, such as biotite granite, crystal granite, fine-grained, coarse-grained, porphyritic granite or granite from various sites.

The identification system in this book

The identification system developed for this book should help you t overcome all difficulties in recognising and naming rocks. There ar 70 colour photos showing typical specimens of all important rocks the most important rocks (e.g. granite, gneiss and limestone) are represented in a number of illustrations to show their various formations. The rocks are classified in four groups (plutonic, extrusive sedimentary and metamorphic), each indicated by a coloured stripe:

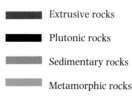

Extrusive rocks

Plutonic rocks

Sedimentary rocks

Metamorphic rocks

4

The groups correspond to the three main sequences in which rocks are classified by origin.

The *igneous* sequence includes all rocks produced from molten rock (magma). If the molten rock solidified inside the earth, the corresponding rocks are called *plutonic* (or intrusive), e.g. granite, diorite and syenite. These are marked by a *black stripe*. If the rock solidified at or close under the surface, it is called *extrusive* (or volcanic), e.g. basalt, andesite and rhyolite. These are marked by a *red stripe*.

The *sedimentary* sequence includes rocks produced by physical or chemical processes: weathering, transport and deposition (sedimentation); e.g. sand, sandstone and limestone. These are marked by a *blue stripe*.

The *metamorphic* sequence includes rocks produced from other rocks by pressure and/or temperature change, e.g. mica schist, gneiss and eclogite. These are marked by a *green stripe*.

The place referred to in the caption is where the stone in the picture was discovered. The scale is indicated, giving you an exact idea of actual size. Technical terms used in the descriptive notes are explained in the Glossary following this Introduction.

Identification procedure

1 Find the group to which the rock belongs, by comparing it with the illustrations on the front and back inside covers, which show the typical structural features of the various types of rock.
Note the difference between plutonic and extrusive rock: extrusive rock, unlike plutonic, nearly always has an extremely fine-grained matrix.
2 Now determine the main constituents of the rock, i.e. the minerals which the rock contains. Information about the minerals in a rock will provide one of the most important starting-points in identification. However, minerals in rocks are difficult to identify because they are often very small and usually not crystalline.
3 You can distinguish marble and limestone from other rocks by the HCl test (see the following Glossary). They effervesce when treated with acid.
4 Now concentrate on one of the main constituents you have found (i.e. the one present in the largest proportion if recognisable), and compare all the rocks in the group identified in paragraph 1, which have the corresponding mineral as the main constituent.
5 Out of this group, find the rocks which also contain the other main constituents you have found.
6 In most cases you will now have identified the rock. If you still have a number of rocks to choose from, look under the heading

Similar rocks, showing how they differ from the rock illustrated. You will obtain additional hints from **Occurrence**.

7 The external shape of the rock, often altered by wind or water, should not be taken as a guide to identification. In the illustration below, the irregularly broken specimen belongs to the same species as the smooth round pebble. It is also very rare for colour to be a guide to the species under which the specimen should be classified.

Glossary

Words in italics can be found elsewhere in the Glossary.

Anatexis: the end stage of *metamorphism* i.e. partial melting of the rock. When the temperature rises further the rock completely re-melts and forms a *magma*. This process is called palingenesis.

Annular: in the form of a ring.

Basalt columns: polygonal columns produced by the cooling of outpourings of basalt.

Batholith: see *Intrusion*.

Caves: large cavities in the rock, particularly common in carbonate and sulphate rocks. Often caused by flowing water which dissolves the rock. In areas of limestone, water may flow through large caves or drip, causing stalactites and deposits of travertine.

Chimney: a vent of a volcano, or the plug that has filled such a vent.

Conchoidal: shell-shaped, describing the shape of the fracture produced when obsidian and some other rocks are broken.

Concretion: a concentration of minerals, often in a sphere, contained within the *sedimentary rock* of an area.

Conformable: describes parallel undisturbed strata lying one above the other. Strata at an angle and intersecting the flat strata rest unconformably.

Constituents: the species of mineral making up the rock. The main species form a large percentage of the rock, minor constituents 1% or less.

Contact metamorphism: the alteration of rocks caused by contact with a body of *igneous rock*.

Country rock: the ordinary rock characteristic of an area, used particularly to contrast it with any intrusions, *gangues*, etc.

Crust: the 'solid' outer part of the earth, as opposed to the molten interior.

Crystallisation: the time during which a *magma* crystallises. It may be divided into early, main and residual stages.

Diagenesis: solidification of loose sediment under the pressure of overhead strata. Diagenesis merges into the lowest stages of *metamorphism*.

Dome: an *intrusion* of *igneous rocks* with a roof shaped like a dome.

Ejecta: solid material ejected by volcanoes.

Equigranular: having mineral grains which are all of about equal size.

Extrusion: an emergence of molten rock onto the surface of the earth.

Extrusive ridge: rocks formed from the solidification of molten rock which has cooled on the surface of the earth.

Facies: all the features of a rock. The metamorphic facies is important in mineralogy, since the association of minerals in the rock can be used to classify it in a particular range of metamorphism.

Flow structure: if the components of a rock, when fluid, become so arranged as to indicate the direction of flow of the melt, and this is still recognisable when the rock has solidified, a flow structure can be seen.

Folding: the bending and distortion of originally flat layers of *sedimentary rock*, and the structures that form through this process.

Fossils: petrified remains of animals and plants.

Fumarole: a gaseous eruption from an active volcano. Gases escaping from quiescent volcanoes are called solfataras. The best-known solfatara is that at Pozzuoli near Naples.

Gangue: fills a cleft in rock with minerals which are more recent than the rock. The perforated rock is called *country rock*, and the gangue boundary is called the wall.

Gangue rocks: rocks filling clefts in other rocks. The gangue can be up to several kilometres thick and over 100 kilometres long.

Geochemistry: that branch of geology concerned with the distribution and frequency of chemical elements in the earth's crust. In this sense the crust includes not only minerals and rocks but also earth, water and air. Geochemistry can also include all chemical reactions having any relation to geological processes. In general, the 'geochemistry' of a stone means its contents of chemical elements.

Grain boundary: the boundary between two intergrown mineral grains. At the boundary the mechanical strength is lowest, and consequently *weathering* generally begins there.

Gravel: a loose rock with particle sizes between 2mm and 2cm.

Green schist, greenstone: general terms applied to low-grade *metamorphic* rocks characterised by their content of epidote, chlorite and other green minerals. They are usually produced from gabbros or other basic rocks.

HCl test: in this, the rock under test is wetted with hydrochloric acid (HCl) to see whether it gives off carbon dioxide (effervesces).

Igneous rocks: have their origin as molten rock (magma) within the earth. If they solidify inside the earth they are plutonic (intrusive). If they solidify at the surface they are extrusive.

Impregnation: filling of very fine cavities in a rock with a more recent mineral.

Intrusion: penetration of molten rock into any parts of the earth's crust. The intrusion bodies produced when the melt solidifies are called plutons. Large round plutons are also called batholiths.

Intrusive rocks: an alternative name for *Plutonic rocks*.

Joints: cavities produced by tension in the rock. They can be filled wholly or partly with mineral formations.

Lamellar: with a leaf-like or plate-like structure.

Lava: molten rock emerging at the earth's surface. It solidifies into *extrusive rocks*. Depending on its chemical composition, lava may be viscous or free-flowing.

Lens: a more or less lens-shaped body of rock within another type of rock.

Macroscopic: visible with the naked eye.

Magma: molten rock inside the earth. When it soldifies it produces *igneous rocks*.

Mantlerock: a layer of loose rock (including soil and sediments) resting on solid rock and forming the land surface.

Marl: limestone with a high clay content and only slightly agglomerated.

Massif: a concentrated group of mountain heights.

Matrix: the ground material of a rock within which crystals and other inclusions lie.

Metamorphic rocks: rocks produced by metamorphism.

Metamorphism: the conversion of rocks under heat and/or pressure. In *contact metamorphism* high temperatures from *magma* cause the changes. This produces minerals such as vesuvianite, garnet, diopside, andalusite, etc. In *regional metamorphism* the rock sinks to greater depth, resulting in increased pressure and temperature and producing rocks such as gneiss, mica-schist or crystalline schist.

Oolitic: describes rocks made up of spheres with a concentric structure (oolites). They are produced in surf by deposition of calcite or iron or manganese oxides round sand grains or other particles.

Palingenesis: see *Anatexis*.

Phenocryst: a crystal embedded in a finer-grained matrix. This is called a porphyritic structure and usually occurs in *igneous rocks*.

Plagioclase: any of a series of feldspar minerals, such as anorthite and labradorite, found in igneous and metamorphic rocks.

Pluton: see *Intrusion*.

Plutonic rocks: rocks formed from the solidification of molten rock which has cooled inside the earth.

Porphyritic: see *Phenocryst*.

Regional metamorphism: changes in texture and minerals in rocks subjected to compression and shearing in earth movements, with consequent rises in temperature.

Retrograde metamorphism: occurs under falling temperatures and pressures. In the process, high pressure and temperature minerals are converted into minerals stable at lower temperatures and pressures.

Rock: a large geological body (from metres to kilometres in size) made up of minerals. A rock may consist of one species of mineral (marble, quartzite) or a number (granite, gneiss, gabbro).

Rock glass: produced when molten rock cools so fast that its components do not crystallise but instead form a glassy mass.

Sand: a loose rock consisting mainly of quartz grains below 2mm in size.

Schistous: with a tendency to split along planes of weakness.

Schlieren: striations or streaks within a rock.

Sedimentary rocks: rocks which are often fairly fine-grained, formed by weathering, transport by wind or water, and subsequent redeposition. They can also be formed by precipitation of dissolved substances. They can be loose (sand, gravel) or solid (limestone, sandstone). They are often stratified and can contain animal and plant remains.

Sequence: a development series for minerals and rocks. The igneous sequence includes minerals and rocks formed from *magma*, the sedimentary sequence includes minerals and rocks produced by chemical or physical weathering and sedimentation, and so on.

Shale: a smooth, fine-grained sedimentary rock, formed by the compression of layers of clay, that splits easily into thin parallel layers or flakes.

Skarn: a rock produced by contact between silicon-rich molten material and limestone rocks.

Stalagmites: structures formed in caverns by the precipitation of calcium carbonate from dripping water in limestone areas. Stalagmites are conical structures which continually grow upward. Hanging cones growing down from the roof are stalactites. Both are 'dripstones'. They occur in a wide variety of forms and may imitate plants, animals, buildings and so on.

Strata: the layers that are visible in sedimentary rock.

Stratification: deposition of sedimentary strata with differences in the homogeneity of the particles. A rock consisting of completely similar particles cannot be stratified. Stratification can be *conformable* or unconformable.

Subduction zone: the region where one of the plates of the earth's crust is being pushed under another.

Terrestrial: structures produced on solid land, e.g. dunes or rockslides.

Ultrabasic rocks: very basic rocks consisting mainly of olivine, pyroxene, amphibole and biotite.

Volcanic ash: fine particles of loose material ejected by volcanoes.

Volcanic rocks: an alternative name for *Extrusive rocks*.

Volcanic slag: porous, coagulated volcanic ejecta.

Weathering: destruction of a mineral or rock by chemical, physical or biological factors.

Rhyolite

Picture: Light-coloured rhyolite with fine-grained matrix and large phenocrysts of sanidine. Found at: La Bourbante, French Massif Central. Half-size.

Main constituents: Quartz, potassium feldspar. **Minor constituents:** Plagioclase (albite), biotite. **Appearance:** Very light-coloured; very finely crystalline matrix with phenocrysts of sanidine (potassium feldspar) and quartz, frequent flow structures. **Origin:** On emergence of high-silica magmas; is the extrusive rock corresponding to granite. **Occurrence:** In chimneys, massifs and gangues, or surface extrusions often covering large areas. **Found in:** Devon; Cornwall; Wales; Lipari Islands, Italy. **Similar rocks:** Dacite contains larger quantities of plagioclase (labradorite-oligoclase); trachyte and latite contain pyroxenes as the main constituents.

Rhyolite

Picture: Quartz porphyry (geologically old rhyolite) with fine-grained matrix coloured red by iron and larger phenocrysts of quartz and potassium feldspar. Found at: Kastelruth, South Tirol. Half-size.

Dacite

Picture: Dacite with fine-grained matrix and phenocrysts of plagioclase and hornblende. Found at: Sacaramb, Siebenbürgen, Romania. Half-size.

Main constituents: Plagioclase (labradorite-oligoclase), quartz, potassium feldspar. **Minor constituents:** Biotite, hornblende, pyroxene. **Appearance:** Light to medium-grey; matrix extremely fine-grained, often glassy, phenocrysts of plagioclase, quartz, occasionally biotite, hornblende, frequent flow structures. **Origin:** On emergence of high-silica magmas; is the extrusive rock corresponding to tonalite. **Occurrence:** In chimneys, massifs, mantlerock. **Found in:** Scotland; Puy de Dôme, France. **Similar rocks:** Andesite contains no quartz, rhyolite contains plagioclase with less anorthite.

Latite

Picture: Fine-grained grey quartz latite. Found at: Stenzelberg, Siebengebirge, Germany. Half-size.

Main constituents: Plagioclase (labradorite-andesine), sanidine, pyroxene. **Minor constituents:** Hornblende, biotite. **Appearance:** Light to medium-grey. Very fine-grained, often glassy matrix. Phenocrysts of plagioclase, pyroxene, sanidine, sometimes flow structures. **Origin:** On emergence of monzonitic magmas; is the extrusive rock corresponding to monzonite. **Occurrence:** In lava-flows, mantlerocks, gangues. **Found in:** Canary Is; Puy de Dôme, France; Latium, Italy. **Similar rocks:** Dacite and rhyolite contain quartz; andesite contains no potassium feldspar; trachyte contains plagioclase with less anorthite.

Andesite

Picture: Andesite with fine-grained matrix and larger phenocrysts of hornblende and augite. Found at: Deva, Hungary. Half-size.

Main constituents: Plagioclase (labradorite-andesine), pyroxene, hornblende. **Minor constituents:** Biotite, magnetite. **Appearance:** Brown to brown-black; fine-grained matrix, sometimes glassy, phenocrysts of plagioclase, pyroxene, hornblende, usually very small, rarely over 1 cm in size. **Origin:** On melting of oceanic crusts in subduction zones. **Occurrence:** As lava-flows, massifs, domes. **Found in:** Cumberland; Euganean Hills, Italy. **Similar rocks:** Dacite and rhyolite contain quartz; latite contains sanidine. The different varieties are named after the phenocrysts, e.g. hornblende-andesite.

Andesite

Picture: Hornblende-andesite with fine-grained matrix and especially large phenocrysts of hornblende and plagioclase. Found at Krivelje near Bor, Yugoslavia. Half-size.

Basalt

Picture: Analcime basalt with fine-grained matrix and phenocrysts of analcime which decompose in sunlight, so that this basalt is called 'Sunburner'. Found at: Römlinghoven, Siebengebirge, Germany. Half-size.

Main constituents: Plagioclase (labradorite-anorthite), pyroxene, magnetite. **Minor constituents:** Olivine, hornblende, biotite.
Appearance: Black to grey-black, black-brown; dense, conchoidal structure, also slaggy, with rough surface, very fine-grained matrix, usually few phenocrysts of plagioclase, pyroxene, olivine. **Origin:** On emergence of gabbroid magmas. **Occurrence:** In lava streams, mantlerock (where it often makes polygonal columns, formed during cooling), massifs, gangues. **Use:** As street metal, paving-stones.
Found in: Mull and Staffa, Scotland; Northern Ireland; Etna, Sicily;

Basalt

Picture: Nepheline basalt with fine-grained matrix and larger phenocrysts of nepheline, which however are difficult to recognise. Found at: Forst, Rhine Palatinate, Germany. Half-size.

Hekla, Iceland. **Similar rocks:** Basalt varies greatly in mineral composition, resulting in a number of varieties which are not easy to distinguish macroscopically. Owing to its typical appearance, however, this group is easy to distinguish from other rocks.

Trachyte

Picture: Grey trachyte with fine-grained matrix and larger phenocrysts of sanidine. Found at: Laacher See, Eifel, Germany. One-third size.

Main constituents: Sanidine, plagioclase (andesine). **Minor constituents:** Biotite, amphibole, pyroxene. **Appearance:** White to light grey; fine-grained matrix, large phenocrysts of sanidine, usually parallel, flow structures, porous, with rough surface. **Origin:** On emergence of syenitic magmas; is the extrusive rock corresponding to syenite. **Occurrence:** In lava streams, massifs, domes. **Similar rocks:** Latite contains plagioclase richer in anorthite; dacite and rhyolite contain quartz; andesite contains no sanidine.

Obsidian

Picture: Black glassy obsidian without phenocrysts. Found at: Štam Dagh, Yerevan, USSR. Half-size.

Main constituent: Rock glass. **Minor constituents:** Cristobalite, magnetite. **Appearance:** Black, brown, greenish, glassy-dense with few phenocrysts, transparent to opaque, conchoidal fracture. **Origin:** On very rapid cooling of magmas, particularly when rich in silicon. **Occurrence:** Crusts on lava; ejecta. **Use:** In the Stone Age, tools were produced from obsidian. **Found:** In almost all recent lava intrusions, e.g. Lipari Islands, Italy, and Etna, Sicily. **Similar rocks:** unmistakable, owing to its glassy appearance.

Phonolite

Picture: Light-coloured fine-grained selbergite (noselite-phonolite) with larger phenocrysts of noselite. Found at: Schellkopf, Brenk, Germany. Half-size.

Main constituents: Nephelinĕ, potassium feldspar (sanidine), aegirine. **Minor constituents:** Noselite, hauynite, sodalite, olivine, melanite, sodium hornblende. **Appearance:** Light to dark grey, brown, greenish; fine-grained with phenocrysts of sanidine, hauynite, nepheline, typical conchoidal fracture, gives a clear sound when struck ('clinkstone'), frequent flow structures. **Origin:** From alkali-rich magmas; is the extrusive rock corresponding to nepheline syenite. **Occurrence:** As volcanic massifs; also in gangue (tinguaite). **Use:** as building-material. **Found in:** Scotland; Cornwall. **Similar rocks:** Tephrite contains leucite in addition, and has

Phonolite

Picture: Fine-grained phonolite with larger phenocrysts of potassium feldspar and aegirine. Found at: Kirchweiler, Kaiserstuhl, Germany. Half-size.

different content of clearly-visible nepheline.

Tephrite

Picture: Fine-grained limburgite with larger phenocrysts of augite and many cavities. Found at: Limburg, Kaiserstuhl, Germany. One-third size.

Main constituents: Plagioclase (labradorite-bytownite), monoclinic pyroxene. **Minor constituents:** Nepheline, leucite, amphibole, biotite. **Appearance:** Grey to black; often porous, fine-grained with phenocrysts (leucite, plagioclase); frequent cavities filled with later minerals (calcite, aragonite, zeolites). **Origin:** From basic lava, often through resorption of carbonate rocks. **Occurrence:** in extrusions, gangues. **Similar rocks:** The complete absence of potassium feldspar is characteristic. Basanite also contains olivine.

Tephrite

Picture: Fine-grained leucite tephrite with large ingrown leucite crystals. Found at: Capo di Bove, Rome. Half-size.

Leucitite

Picture: Leucitite with large leucite crystals cemented by a fine-grained matrix of pyroxene and olivine. Found at: Lago di Bracciano, Latium, Italy. Half-size.

Main constituent: Leucite. **Minor constituents:** Pyroxene, olivine, melilite. **Appearance:** White to light grey; fine-grained matrix, many phenocrysts of leucite, often porous with cavities. **Origin:** From magmas undersaturated with silica, which have often resorbed country rock. **Occurrence:** In gangues and lava streams. **Similar rocks:** The large phenocrysts of leucite are typical. Tephrite and basanite also contain plagioclase.

Nephelinite

Picture: Coarse-grained nephelinite with large nepheline phenocrysts. Found at: Melches, Vogelsberg, Germany. Half-size.

Main constituent: Nepheline. **Minor constituents:** Olivine, pyroxene, melilite, perovskite. **Appearance:** Light to medium grey; fine-grained matrix with phenocrysts of nepheline, pyroxene, often porous. **Origin:** From magmas very undersaturated with silica. **Occurrence:** As massifs, gangues. **Similar rocks:** Phonolite also contains sanidine.

Pumice

Picture: Foamy pumice with many cavities and fibrous structure with small sanidine phenocrysts. Found at: Furnas, Azores. Half-size.

Main constituent: Rock glass. **Minor constituents:** Sanidine, hornblende, pyroxene. **Appearance:** White to light grey; spongy, with many cavities, very light, floats on water. **Origin:** In volcanic eruptions rich in gas. **Occurrence:** In strata, in ejecta of volcanoes rich in silica. **Use:** For producing light building materials. **Found in:** Italy; Canary Is. **Similar rocks:** Owing to its low specific gravity it cannot be mistaken.

Volcanic tuff

Picture: Phonolite tuff with constituents of greatly varying size, irregularly coagulated. Found at: Hohentwiel, Hegau, Germany. Half-size.

Constituents: Volcanic ejecta, volcanic ash, rock glass, augite. **Appearance:** Grey, brown; wide range of particle sizes, porous, frequent larger phenocrysts of augite, hornblende, biotite or sanidine crystals, often very finely stratified. **Origin:** Through deposition and solidification of loose material ejected by volcanoes. **Occurrence:** Around volcanoes. **Use:** Sometimes as building material. **Found in:** Lake District; North Wales; Vesuvius, Naples, Italy; Etna, Sicily. **Similar rocks:** Travertine effervesces when dipped in dilute hydrochloric acid.

Granite

Picture: Fine-grained granite with red potassium feldspar, biotite and muscovite. Found at: Roland Mine, Wölsendorf, Germany. Half-size.

Main constituents: Potassium feldspar, plagioclase (albite-oligoclase), quartz. **Minor constituents:** Biotite, muscovite, hornblende, pyroxene, tourmaline. Depending on the minor constituents there are many varieties: biotite granite, muscovite granite, two-mica granite, hornblende granite, tourmaline granite. **Appearance:** White, grey, reddish, greenish; medium to coarse-grained, often porphyritic with large potassium feldspar crystals, frequent inclusions of foreign rocks which are often completely resorbed (converted into biotite). **Origin:** Melting of sediments of overall granitic chemical make-up, as the last stage of metamor-

Granite

Picture: Fine-grained biotite granite with large white potassium feldspar crystals. Found at: Gavorrano, Tuscany. Half-size.

phism (palingenesis); from juvenile magmas from the interior of the earth. **Occurrence:** Forms small to large intrusions with considerable contact with country rock, massifs, domes, gangues. **Use:** As building material; road-construction; road-metal; facade lining; tombstones. **Found in:** Scotland; Lake District; Cornwall. Granite is an extremely widespread rock. **Similar rocks:** Alkali granite contains only potassium feldspar. In granodiorite the plagioclase predominates over potassium feldspar. Tonalite contains plagioclase as the only feldspar.

Granite

Picture: Crystal granite with fine-grained matrix and large phenocrysts of potassium feldspar. Found at: Bergell, Switzerland. Half-size.

Main constituents: Potassium feldspar, plagioclase (albite-oligoclase), quartz. **Minor constituents:** Biotite, muscovite, hornblende, pyroxene, tourmaline. **Appearance:** White, grey, reddish, greenish; medium to coarse-grained, often porphyritic with large potassium feldspar crystal; frequent inclusions of foreign rocks which are often completely resorbed. **Origin:** Melting of sediments of overall granitic chemical make-up, as the last stage of metamorphism (palingenesis); from juvenile magmas from the interior of the earth. **Occurrence:** Forms small to large intrusions with considerable contact with country rock, massifs, gangues.

Tonalite

Picture: Medium-grained tonalite with clearly visible phenocrysts of hornblende. Found at: Lake Garda, Italy. Half-size.

Main constituents: Plagioclase (oligoclase-andesine), quartz, hornblende. **Minor constituents:** Biotite, rarely muscovite, pyroxene. **Appearance:** Light to dark grey, often light with dark phenocrysts (hornblende, biotite); medium to coarse-grained. **Origin:** Melting of rocks at great depths. **Occurrence:** In large granitic intrusion bodies. **Use:** as building material. **Found in:** Scotland. **Similar rocks:** Granodiorite, granite and alkali granite contain potassium feldspar.

Monzonite

Picture: Fine-grained brown monzonite from the place which gave it its name. Found at: Monzoni, Predazzo, Italy. Half-size.

Main constituents: Plagioclase (labradorite), potassium feldspar, pyroxene. **Minor constituents:** Quartz, biotite. **Appearance:** Light to dark grey, greenish, brownish; medium-grained, frequent flow structures. **Origin:** Through local remelting. **Occurrence:** In small intrusion bodies, massifs, lenses. **Found at:** Isle of Skye, Scotland. **Similar rocks:** Syenite contains more potassium feldspar and plagioclases richer in sodium (andesine); gabbro and norite contain no potassium feldspar.

Syenite

Picture: Coarse-grained hornblende syenite with phenocrysts of hornblende. Found at: Senones, Vosges, France. Half-size.

Main constituents: Potassium feldspar, plagioclase (andesine-oligoclase), hornblende. **Minor constituents:** Biotite, pyroxene, quartz. **Appearance:** Light to dark grey; medium to coarse-grained, occasionally porphyritic, often with cavities, porous. **Origin:** Through differentiation from more basic magmas. **Occurrence:** In small independent intrusive bodies; in differentiated gabbro intrusions. **Found in:** Scotland. **Similar rocks:** Granite has quartz as main constituent; diorite contains practically no potassium feldspar.

Diorite

Picture: Fine-grained titanite-spotted diorite with phenocrysts of titanite always surrounded by a white area in which the black constituents are missing. Found at: Schlägl, Upper Austria. One-third size.

Main constituents: Plagioclase (oligoclase-andesine), hornblende. **Minor constituents:** Quartz, biotite, pyroxene. **Appearance:** Medium to dark grey, blackish; fine to medium-grained, sometimes porphyritic, occasionally spherical structure (spherical diorite). **Origin:** On differentiation of granitic magmas as first precipitate. **Occurrence:** As boundary facies of large acid intrusions; in small independent intrusions. **Found in:** Scotland; Channel Is. **Similar rocks:** Gabbro contains anorthite-rich plagioclase and pyroxene as the main constituent.

Diorite

Structure: Medium-grained mica diorite with larger phenocrysts of biotite. Found at: Gerhardts Quarry, Waldviertel, Germany. Half-size.

Gabbro

Picture: Coarse-grained gabbro with large individual dual crystals of pyroxene and plagioclase. Also called troutstone, owing to its appearance. Found at: Bombiani, Italy. Half-size.

Main constituents: Plagioclase (labradorite-bytownite), monoclinic pyroxene. **Minor constituents:** Ilmenite, magnetite, hornblende, olivine. **Appearance:** Medium to dark grey, light to dark green, black-brown; medium to coarse-grained, sometimes porphyritic, often streaked, with flow structures. **Origin:** Through differentiation from ultrabasic magmas in the earth's mantle. **Occurrence:** In large stratified basic intrusions; in independent smaller and larger intrusions. **Found in:** Skye; Arran; Cumbria; Cornwall. **Similar rocks:** Norite is similar except for the occurrence of orthorhombic pyroxenes, which are not easy to detect. Pyroxenite contains

Gabbro

Picture: Very fine-grained gabbro with typical greenish-black colour. Found at Harzburg, Harz, Germany. Half-size.

practically no plagioclase. Anorthosite contains practically no pyroxene.

Essexite

Picture: Fine-grained essexite with pyroxene phenocrysts. Found at: Crawfordjohn, Scotland. Half-size.

Main constituents: Plagioclase (labradorite), potassium feldspar, pyroxene, the plagioclase predominating over the feldspar. **Minor constituents:** Sodalite, noselite, leucite, hornblende, nepheline, biotite. **Appearance:** Dark-grey to black; fine to medium-grained, sometimes with plagioclase phenocrysts. **Origin:** From strongly alkaline magmas. **Occurrence:** In small intrusions, often together with other alkaline rocks. **Use:** For curling stones. **Found in:** Scotland. **Similar rocks:** Monzonite contains roughly equal amounts of plagioclase and potassium feldspar; nepheline-syenite contains no labradorite.

Nepheline-syenite

Picture: Coarse-grained nepheline-syenite with much potassium feldspar and black amphibole. Found at: Langesundfjord, Norway. Half-size.

Main constituents: Potassium feldspar, albite, nepheline. **Minor constituents:** Pyroxenes, amphiboles, olivine, melanite, cancrinite, sodalite. **Appearance:** Light-coloured, white, yellowish, brownish, occasionally dark; medium to coarse-grained. **Origin:** From very alkaline magmas. **Occurrence:** In annual intrusion bodies, alone or with other alkaline rocks. **Similar rocks:** Cannot be mistaken, owing to characteristic appearance of nepheline grains.

Pyroxenite

Picture: Coarse-grained pyroxenite with bronzite as main constituent. Found at: Webster County, North Carolina, USA. Half-size.

Main constituents: Orthorhombic pyroxene, monoclinic pyroxene. **Minor constituents:** Chromite, hornblende, spinel, titanite, apatite, perovskite. **Appearance:** Brown to black, black-green; often widely varied granulation. **Origin:** On differentiation of basic magmas. **Occurrence:** In basic magmatic series of strata; in small independent intrusions; as volcanic ejecta. **Similar rocks:** Cannot be mistaken, since pyroxenes are the only main constituents.

Peridotite

Picture: Fine-grained peridotite with large garnet phenocrysts. Found at: Alpe Arami, Ticino, Switzerland. Half-size.

Main constituents: Olivine, pyroxene. **Minor constituents:** Spinel, hornblende, chromite, garnet, phlogopite. **Appearance:** Light to dark green; medium-grained. **Origin:** On differentiation of basic magmas. **Occurrence:** At the base of series of magmatic strata; as inclusions in basalt; as smaller independent intrusions. **Found in:** Lizard, Cornwall. **Similar rocks:** Dunite has no major constituents apart from olivine.

Anorthosite

Picture: Coarse-grained black-brown anorthosite with iridescent blue labradorite feldspar. Found at: Lac St. Jean, Quebec, Canada. Half-size.

Main constituent: Plagioclase (labradorite-bytownite). **Minor constituents:** Pyroxene, olivine, chromite, magnetite. **Appearance:** White, grey, blackish, greenish, reddish; medium to coarse-grained, equigranular. **Origin:** On differentiation of basic magmas. **Occurrence:** As strata, layers inside basic intrusion complexes. **Use:** As ornamental stone (gravestones, facades). **Similar rocks:** Cannot be mistaken, owing to almost mono-mineral composition of plagioclases rich in anorthite.

Aplite

Picture: Fine-grained light granite aplite as gangue in medium-grained biotite granite. Found at: Jahreiss Quarry, Tittling, Germany. One-third size.

Main constituents: Quartz, potassium feldspar. **Minor constituents:** Biotite, muscovite, tourmaline, hornblende. **Appearance:** White to light-grey; fine-grained, sometimes in zones. **Origin:** At end of crystallisation of intrusions. **Occurrence:** As gangues. **Found at:** Aplite occurs in all granite areas. **Similar rocks:** Pegmatite is much coarser-grained.

Pegmatite

Picture: Pegmatite with quartz and red potassium feldspar, small joint partly filled with quartz. Found at: Hermine Mine, Wölsendorf, Germany. One-third size.

Main constituents: Quartz, potassium feldspar, plagioclase. **Minor constituents:** Biotite, muscovite, lepidolite and many others. **Appearance:** Very varied colour; extremely coarse-grained, often with cavities. **Origin:** At end of mass crystallisation of rocks. **Occurrence:** As gangues, massifs, schlieren, usually in granite sequence. **Use:** For obtaining feldspar, quartz, etc. **Similar rocks:** The coarse grains are unmistakable. Aplite is finer-grained.

Carbonatite

Picture: Coarse-grained carbonatite with large phlogopite phenocrysts. Found at: Sud Ås, Sweden. Half-size.

Main constituents: Calcspar, dolomite. **Minor constituents:** Phlogopite, apatite, nepheline, perovskite, monazite, barytes, pyrochlore. **Appearance:** White, yellowish, grey, brown; medium to coarse-grained. **Origin:** From fused carbonates from the lower mantle. **Occurrence:** In massifs and gangues inside alkaline rock complexes; extrusions of carbonatite lava have also been observed (Oldoinyo Lengai, Tanzania). **Similar rocks:** Marble does not usually occur with alkaline rocks.

Lamprophyre

Picture: Fine-grained kersantite with predominating plagioclase. Found at: Kropfmühl near Hauzenberg, Bavarian Forest, Germany. Half-size.

Main constituents: Biotite, hornblende, potassium feldspar, plagioclase (labradorite). **Minor constituents:** Pyroxene, olivine. **Appearance:** Dark-grey, dark-brown to black; fine-grained, sometimes porphyritic with biotite or hornblende phenocrysts. **Origin:** At end of crystallisation of larger intrusions. **Occurrence:** In gangues and clefts in the sequence of granitic to gabbroid rocks. **Found in:** Jersey; Lake District; all larger intrusion complexes. **Similar rocks:** Dark plutonic rocks are unmistakable, but it is not easy to distinguish members of the group.

Sandstone

Picture: Bunter or mottled sandstone with cross-stratification.
Found at: Upper Neckar, Germany. One-third size.

Main constituent: Quartz grains. **Minor constituents:** Mica, feldspar, calcspar, heavy minerals; quartz or calcspar binder. **Appearance:** White, light to dark grey, brown; fine to medium-grained, often stratified. **Origin:** From erosion residues of crystalline rocks. **Occurrence:** In all strata sequences; always near Continent. **Found in:** Cheshire; S. England; extremely widespread. **Similar rocks:** Arkose contains feldspar; greywacke also contains rock fragments as the main constituents.

Arkose

Picture: Irregular-grained arkose, coloured red by iron oxides; clearly visible feldspar fragments. Found at: Wernberg, Schmidgaden, Germany. Half-size.

Constituents: Grains of quartz, feldspar, mica. **Appearance:** Light to dark-grey, yellowish, reddish; medium-grained, often irregular grains, sometimes stratified. **Origin:** Weathering of plutonic rocks; the transport distance must be short enough not to destroy the feldspar. **Occurrence:** In fresh and salt-water deposits beside larger crystalline complexes; always near coast. **Found in:** Scotland. **Similar rocks:** Sandstone contains no feldspar grains; greywacke also contains rock fragments.

Breccia

Picture: Breccia of angular fragments of weathered limestone. Found at: Partnachklamm near Garmisch-Partenkirchen, Germany. Half-size.

Constituents: Non-rounded rock fragments, sandy, lime or clay binder. **Appearance:** Very varied colour; coarse-grained, often with very varied particle sizes. **Origin:** Mechanical destruction of rocks and subsequent re-solidification without further transport. **Occurrence:** In areas with strong mechanical movement of rock. **Found in:** Scotland; W. England; usually with narrow local limits. **Similar rocks:** Conglomerates consist of rounded rock fragments.

Conglomerate

Picture: Nagelfluh, a conglomerate with variously-sized rounded fragments of various rocks with lime or clay binder. Found at: Talmühle near Traunwalchen, Traunreuth, Germany. Half-size.

Constituents: Rounded gravel or shingle, lime-clay binder, sandy. **Appearance:** Great variety of colour; coarse-grained, often with very different particle sizes, sometimes stratified. **Origin:** Through solidification of river and sea shingle. **Occurrence:** In fresh-water and sea sediments. **Found in:** Scotland; London Basin. **Similar rocks:** Breccia consists of angular rock fragments.

Limestone

Picture: Bituminous lime marl with layers of concentrated organic substances. Found at: Marienstein Cement Works. One-third size.

Main constituent: Calcspar. **Minor constituents:** Limonite, dolomite, quartz, organic substances. **Appearance:** White, yellowish, brownish, grey, black; fine to coarse-grained, in layers or blocks, can often be split into plates, often contains many fossils, may consist of up to 100% fossil remains (e.g. mussel shells). **Origin:** Usually organic, from lime produced by living organisms; more rarely through inorganic precipitation. **Occurrence:** Limestones are extremely widespread in all sedimentary strata sequences. **Found in:** S. England; Midlands.

Limestone

Picture: Siliceous limestone with high quartz content, shown by inclusion of many flint nodules. Found at: Bopfingen, Swabian Jura, Germany. Half-size.

Main constituent: Calcspar. **Minor constituents:** Limonite, dolomite, quartz, organic substances. **Appearance:** White, yellowish, brownish, grey, black; fine to coarse-grained, in layers or blocks, can often be split into plates, often contains many fossils, may consist of up to 100% fossil remains (e.g. mussel shells). **Origin:** Usually organic, from lime produced by living organisms; more rarely through inorganic precipitation. **Occurrence:** Limestones are extremely widespread in all sedimentary strata sequences. **Use:** Finely coloured, patterned varieties are used as ornamental stone. In the trade they are generally called marble, but this is geologically incor-

Limestone

Picture: Fine-grained, slightly stratified limestone from the Malm, the uppermost Jurassic layer. Found at: Deppenhausen, Swabian Jura, Germany. One-third-size.

...ect, since this name is reserved for metamorphic limestone. **Found in:** Many parts of Britain; widespread. **Similar rocks:** Dolomite does not effervesce with dilute hydrochloric acid; marble differs through its content of metamorphic minerals such as phlogopite.

Limestone

Picture: Bituminous limestone, coloured black by embedded organic substances. More recent white calcspar has filled cracks in the rock. Found at: Poppengrün Quarry, Franconian Forest, Germany. Half-size.

Main constituent: Calcspar. **Minor constituents:** Limonite, dolomite, quartz, organic substances. **Appearance:** White, yellowish, brownish, grey, black; fine to coarse-grained, in layers or blocks, can often be split into plates, often contains many fossils, may consist of up to 100% fossil remains (e.g. mussel shells). **Origin:** Usually organic, from lime produced by living organisms; more rarely through inorganic precipitation. **Occurrence:** Limestones are extremely widespread in all sedimentary strata sequences. **Use:** Finely coloured, patterned varieties are used as ornamental stone. In the

Limestone

Picture: Coral limestone from the Liassic, coloured reddish-brown by iron. The petrified coral appears as white inclusions. Found at: Upper Quarry near Adnet, Austria. Half-size.

trade they are generally called marble, but this is geologically incorrect, since this name is reserved for metamorphic limestone. **Found in:** Britain; widespread. **Similar rocks:** Dolomite does not effervesce with dilute hydrochloric acid; marble differs through its content of metamorphic minerals such as phlogopite.

Limestone

Picture: Very fine-grained limestone or 'chalk'. Found at: Rügen, East Germany. Half-size.

Main constituent: Calcspar. **Minor constituents:** Limonite, dolomite, quartz, organic substances. **Appearance:** White, yellowish, brownish, grey, black; fine to coarse-grained, in layers or blocks, can often be split into plates, often contains many fossils, may consist of up to 100% fossil remains (e.g. mussel shells). **Origin:** Usually organic, from lime produced by living organisms; more rarely through inorganic precipitation. **Occurrence:** Limestones are extremely widespread in all sedimentary strata sequences. **Use:** Finely coloured, patterned varieties are used as ornamental stone. In the trade they are generally called marble, but this is geologically incorrect, since this name is reserved for metamorphic limestone.

Limestone

Picture: Reddish limestone with a number of petrified ammonites, i.e. extinct molluscs related to our cuttle fish. Found at: Schlern, Seiser Alm, Germany. Half-size.

Found in: Britain. Chalk widespread in south (Downs, Chilterns, etc.). **Similar rocks:** Dolomite does not effervesce with dilute hydrochloric acid; marble differs through its content of metamorphic minerals such as phlogopite.

Travertine

Picture: Fresh-water travertine which has formed a crust over organic substances; the print of a leaf is visible. Found at: Pöhl near Murnau, Upper Bavaria, Germany. Half-size.

Main constituent: Calcspar. **Minor constituents:** Limonite, organic substances. **Appearance:** White to brownish; fine-grained to fibrous, very porous, often forms crust around organic substances. **Origin:** Precipitation from lime-rich water. **Occurrence:** At outlet of hot springs; in rivers and streams containing limy water. **Found in:** Derbyshire, etc. **Similar rocks:** Can be distinguished from similar volcanic tuffs by the presence of calcspar as the single main constituent.

Dolomite

Picture: Fine-grained unstratified dolomite from the Triassic. Found at: Heimgarten, Eschenlohe, Germany. One-third size.

Main constituent: Dolomite. **Minor constituents:** Calcspar, limonite, quartz. **Appearance:** White, yellowish, brownish, grey, black; fine to medium-grained, equigranular, sometimes contains fossils. **Origin:** Rarely primary precipitate, usually from limestone through exchange of magnesium with magnesium-containing water or rocks. **Occurrence:** In many sedimentary strata sequences. **Found in:** Dolomites (hence name); NE England. **Similar rocks:** Limestone, unlike dolomite, effervesces when dipped in dilute hydrochloric acid.

Oolitic limestone
'Pea-stone'

Picture: Concentric balls of calcspar, coloured brownish by iron, cemented with calcspar. Found at: Weser Hills, Germany. Half-size.

Main constituents: Calcspar, aragonite. **Minor constituents:** Limonite, chalcedony. **Appearance:** White, brownish; concentric calcspar balls up to 5mm in size, cemented by fine calcspar. **Origin:** In hot springs; chemical precipitation of lime in seawater. **Occurrence:** In deposits from thermal springs; in sedimentary sequences. **Found in:** Cotswolds; Isle of Man; Lake District. **Similar rocks:** Iron oolites consist of limonite and have a different colour.

Coal

Picture: Shiny dense coal. Found at: Peissenberg, Upper Bavaria, Germany. Half-size.

Main constituents: Mineralised organic substances. **Appearance:** Black; 'greasy' shine, conchoidal fracture, flaky, fibrous, dense. **Origin:** Through mineralisation of organic substances of vegetable origin with exclusion of air. **Occurrence:** In seams and layers underneath sedimentary strata sequences. **Use:** As fuel; raw material in the chemical industry. **Found in:** Many areas of Britain. **Similar rocks:** Lignite is browner and much less dense; obsidian is much harder.

Chlorite schist

Picture: Green dense chlorite schist with ingrown, well-formed magnetite octahedra. Found at: Greiner, Zillertal, Austria. One-third size.

Main constituent: Chlorite. **Minor constituents:** Magnetite, pyrite, hornblende, epidote, albite. **Appearance:** Light to dark green; fine to coarse-grained, flaky, schistous, often with magnetite and pyrite phenocrysts. **Origin:** Low-grade regional metamorphism from lava and tuffs and other basic rocks. **Occurrence:** In regional metamorphic areas. **Found in:** Scotland. **Similar rocks:** Mica schist and phyllite have mica as main constituent; amphibolites contain amphiboles as main constituents.

Phyllite

Picture: Black-grey biotite phyllite, partly coloured brown by limonite produced by weathering of iron minerals. Found at: Södring, Lower Austria. One-third size.

Main constituents: Quartz, sericite. **Minor constituents:** Graphite, feldspar, chlorite. **Appearance:** Grey, yellowish, greenish; often silky shine, individual mica flakes indistinguishable with naked eye, schistous, folded. **Origin:** Low-grade regional metamorphism from clay or sandy sediments. **Occurrence:** in regional metamorphic districts. **Found in:** Practically all regional metamorphic districts. **Similar rocks:** Mica schist has individual mica flakes recognisable with the naked eye.

Mica schist

Picture: Silver-grey mica schist with sheaf-like ingrown aggregates of hornblende crystals. Found at: St. Gotthard, Switzerland. Half-size.

Main constituents: Mica, quartz. **Minor constituents:** Feldspar, chlorite, garnet, tourmaline. **Appearance:** Grey, black, brown; fine to coarse-grained, frequent phenocrysts of garnet, tourmaline, kyanite, andalusite, staurolite, stratified, in beds, folded. **Origin:** Medium to high-grade regional metamorphism, clay or sandy rock. **Occurrence:** Frequently in regional metamorphic areas. **Found in:** Scotland. **Similar rocks:** Gneiss also contains feldspar as main constituent; in phyllites the individual mica flakes cannot be distinguished with the naked eye.

Mica schist

Picture: Silver-grey mica schist with large ingrown crystals of garnet. Found at: Stilluptal, Tirol. Half-size.

Gneiss

Picture: Medium-grained equigranular gneiss with two different forms of mica, muscovite and biotite, as constituents. Found at: Unterried, Ötztal, Austria. Half-size.

Main constituents: Feldspar, quartz, mica. **Minor constituents:** Garnet, cordierite, sillimanite, hornblende. **Appearance:** Light to dark grey, brownish, greenish, wide variety of colour; medium to coarse-grained, some phenocrysts of feldspar (augen-gneiss), often schistous with strongly-marked light and dark layers. **Origin:** Medium to high-grade regional metamorphism of clayey sediment (paragneiss) or from granite rocks (orthogneiss). **Occurrence:** Everywhere in regional metamorphic areas. **Use:** As floor or roof tiles. **Found in:** Scotland; W. England. **Similar rocks:** Granite rocks (granite, granodiorite, tonalite) are not schistous.

Gneiss

Picture: Augen-gneiss, a porphyritic gneiss with large feldspar individuals in fine-grained matrix. Found at: Greistal Wind Gap, Zillertal, Austria. Half-size.

Gneiss

Picture: Coarse-grained gneiss with hornblende and plagioclase as main constituents. Found at: Schweinheim, Spessart, Germany. Half-size.

Main constituents: Feldspar, quartz, mica. **Minor constituents:** Garnet, cordierite, sillimanite, hornblende. **Appearance:** Light to dark grey, brownish, greenish, wide variety of colour; medium to coarse-grained, some phenocrysts of feldspar (augen-gneiss), often schistous with strongly-marked light and dark layers. **Origin:** medium to high-grade regional metamorphism of clayey sediment (paragneiss) or from granite rocks (orthogneiss). **Occurrence:** Everywhere in regional metamorphic areas.

Amphibolite

Picture: Dark, massive amphibolite with ingrown garnet crystals. The piece has a lighter, more recent vein of aplite. Found at: Weissenstein, Fichtelgebirge, Germany. Half-size.

Main constituents: Amphibolite (hornblende, actinolite). **Minor constituents:** Epidote, plagioclase, chlorite. **Appearance:** Dark-green to black; coarse-grained, schistous. **Origin:** In low to medium-grade regional metamorphism from basic rocks. **Occurrence:** In regional metamorphic areas. **Similar rocks:** Serpentinites do not contain amphiboles; chlorite schists contain chlorite as the main constituent.

Granulite

Picture: Fine-grained, slightly lamellar granulite with clearly visible garnet phenocrysts. Found at: Marbach, Danube. Half-size.

Main constituents: Potassium feldspar, plagioclase, garnet. **Minor constituents:** Kyanite, cordierite, sillimanite. **Appearance:** White to grey, brownish; fine to coarse-grained, non-lamellar. **Origin:** In high-grade regional metamorphism from sandy or clayey rock. **Occurrence:** In regions of specially high-grade regional metamorphism. **Found in:** NW Scotland. **Similar rocks:** Quartzite does not contain garnet.

Eclogite

Picture: Medium-grained eclogite with red garnet phenocrysts concentrated in schlieren. Found at: Weissenstein, Fichtelgebirge, Germany. One-third size.

Main constituents: Omphacite, garnet. **Minor constituents:** Kyanite, quartz, amphiboles. **Appearance:** Green, sprinkled with red; coarse-grained, often garnet phenocrysts, sometimes stratified. **Origin:** In high-grade regional metamorphism from basic rocks. **Occurrence:** Lenses and beds inside highly metamorphic rock sequences. **Found in:** Scotland. **Similar rocks:** Unmistakable, owing to its characteristic composition.

Marble

Picture: Dolomite marble in which dolomite content predominates over calcspar; typically fine sugar-like structure, which easily crumbles. Found at: Campolungo, Ticino, Switzerland. Half-size.

Main constituent: Calcspar. **Minor constituents:** Dolomite, phlogopite, vesuvianite, wollastonite, diopside, graphite, tremolite. **Appearance:** White, yellowish, brownish; fine to coarse-grained, sometimes in zones. **Origin:** Through regional and contact metamorphism from limestone. **Occurrence:** In the contact zone around metamorphic rock; in regional metamorphic regions. **Use:** For building; ornamental stones; building blocks, but most of the 'marble' on sale is really limestone. The only marble in the mineralogical sense is metamorphic limestone. **Similar rocks:** Carbonatite is without the characteristic minor constituents of

Marble

Picture: Wollastonite skarn with white radiating wollastonite and brown garnet. Found at: Albigna Tunnel, Ivreazone, Italy. Half-size.

marble; gypsum is softer.

Marble

Picture: Coarse-grained marble containing layers of concentrations of dark minerals (graphite, phlogopite). Found at: Holenbrunn, Fichtelgebirge, Germany. Half-size.

Main constituent: Calcspar. **Minor constituents:** Dolomite, phlogopite, vesuvianite, wollastonite, diopside, graphite, tremolite. **Appearance:** White, yellowish, brownish; fine to coarse-grained, sometimes in zones. **Origin:** Through regional and contact metamorphism from limestone. **Occurrence:** In the contact zone around metamorphic rock; in regional metamorphic regions. **Use:** For building; ornamental stones; building blocks, but most of the 'marble' on sale is really limestone. The only marble in the mineralogical sense is metamorphic limestone. **Similar rocks:** Carbonatite is without the characteristic minor constituents of

Marble

Picture: Silicate marble coloured dark by its content of silicate minerals (tremolite, diopside, etc.). The original rock was a very silica-rich limestone. Found at: Spitz, Danube. Half-size.

marble; gypsum is softer.

Foliated schist

Picture: Clay schist from the contact zone of granite with recrystallised andalusite having a dark core (chiastolite). For this reason, this rock is also called chiastolite schist. Found at: Gefrees, Fichtelgebirge, Germany. One-third size.

Main constituents: Mica, quartz, cordierite, andalusite. **Minor constituents:** Magnetite, graphite. **Appearance:** Dark-grey to black; fine-grained with phenocrysts, schistous. **Origin:** Penetration of a pluton into clay schists. **Occurrence:** At outer edge of contact zone around metamorphic rocks. **Similar rocks:** Clay schist does not contain phenocrysts.

Hornfels

Picture: Black hornfels containing a white quartz vein. Found at: Tufidaun, Klausen. Half-size.

Main constituents: Andalusite, cordierite, plagioclase, biotite, hornblende. **Minor constituents:** magnetite, graphite. **Appearance:** brown, black, reddish, violet, greenish; very fine-grained, dense, with conchoidal fracture. **Origin:** Intimate contact between clayey or sandy rocks and metamorphic rock. **Occurrence:** In the inner zone of metamorphic rocks next to an igneous intrusion. **Similar rocks:** Unmistakable, owing to typical conchoidal fracture and occurrence next to ingeneous intrusions.

Quartzite

Picture: Grey-brown fine-grained quartzite; this rock is easily recognisable through its homogeneity and great hardness. Found at: Ebnath, Upper Palatinate, Germany. Half-size.

Main constituent: Quartz. **Minor constituents:** Mica, feldspar, heavy minerals. **Appearance:** White, yellowish, grey; fine-grained, stratified. **Origin:** From high-silica rocks, particularly sandstone, in all stages of metamorphism. **Occurrence:** In many metamorphic strata sequences. **Use:** For producing silica bricks; building material. **Found in:** Scotland. **Similar rocks:** Radiolarite and flinty slate are completely dense, unlike quartzite.

Serpentinite

Picture: 'Precious' serpentine, curved shell-like aggregates with varnish-like surface. Found at: Islitz Falls, Tirol. Half-size.

Main constituents: Serpentine as antigorite, more rarely as chrysotile. **Minor constituents:** Olivine, magnetite, magnesite, talc. **Appearance:** Light to dark green, yellow-green; fine to coarse-grained, felty or flaky, in blocks, often peripherally disintegrated phenocrysts of olivine. **Origin:** Low-grade regional metamorphism from peridotites. **Occurrence:** In regional metamorphic areas. **Found in:** Cornwall. **Similar rocks:** Amphibolite contains amphiboles as the main constituents.

Index of rocks